Introduction

Frontline staff play an absolutely crucial role in the day to day lives of thousands of people who need care and support across the UK.

We know that the work can be extremely demanding, and is not without its stresses, but that it can also be very rewarding.

In recent years, society's expectations of what frontline staff should be doing, and how they should be doing it, have changed dramatically. It is no longer enough simply to 'look after' people; we now have to focus on what each individual person needs and wants, and ensure we provide the kind of service we would be happy to receive ourselves.

Care and support work can raise many issues and dilemmas for frontline staff. Being clear about the purpose of our role, and how we should approach our work, will provide a framework to guide us through these challenges.

Having a clear sense of the principles and values that underpin our work will also help us to think through the challenges, and work out the best way forward.

We hope the booklet will help you identify the simple steps you can take to maintain clear and professional boundaries, and to feel more positive and fulfilled in your role.

Alison Clare
Sharon Lee Cuthbert

In this booklet:

We explain why being clear about the purpose and boundaries of your role is so important.

We describe some simple techniques you can use to put health and social care values into practice.

We provide some examples from our real life experience to illustrate specific points.

There are spaces in each section for you to write down your own responses to key issues, indicated by the '**your thoughts**' button.

Contents

What is the role about?

Key points

If we are clear about our work role we will know where to focus our time and energy.

Being clear about our role means knowing *what* we should be doing as well as *how* we should be doing it.

There may sometimes be a mismatch between what we should be doing and what we actually spend most of our time doing.

Working with people in any job can be challenging. Working with people who need the help of health and social care services can be doubly so. It is very stressful being with people day-in and day-out when they aren't coping or are vulnerable in some way. And providing care and support often means doing personal, sometimes intimate, 'home-like' things with people, although we're at work. The role is demanding and complex. Understanding the care and support role is the first step towards being an effective worker.

A changing role

In the past, care and support workers were often referred to as 'unqualified', 'non-professionally qualified' or 'ancillary' staff. This reflected a common view that they were there to carry out menial tasks at the bidding of the professionally qualified workers.

Consequently, many frontline workers just did what they were told to do and didn't have the opportunity to consider what they were there for.

Care and support work has gained increasing recognition and is now valued as a unique role in its own right. The role is still developing but it is generally recognised that care and support workers:

- work with the everyday issues that are so important to service users
- get to know service users well because they have regular, one-to-one contact
- can share important information about service users to other workers involved in their care and treatment.

The care and support worker plays a central role in promoting people's well-being, which is what health and social care services and interventions are all about. Promoting well-being is about helping people to build up their own internal resources, resilience and strengths to deal with life's ups and downs; to develop meaningful relationships and connections with others, and to do things that they enjoy and that help them feel competent and able.

What do you do in your work to promote the well-being of service users?

List your thoughts here:

1.

2.

3.

Our thoughts about what promoting well-being looks like in practice are on page 33.

In your care and support work role your job title might be something like:

- care assistant
- health care assistant
- support worker
- key worker
- outreach worker
- floating support worker
- personal assistant
- home carer
- support, time and recovery (STR) worker.

Professional v frontline roles

It takes many years of specialist training to achieve a professional level of knowledge and skills in a specific field. Consequently, the qualified professional tends to be seen as 'expert' and the service user as 'their patient'. Most service users have very little contact with these specialists and they generally see them only occasionally and for short periods of time.

In contrast, the relationship between care and support workers and service users is much more equal. They are not experts who diagnose problems or tell service users what to do. They work alongside people and have the opportunity to form a working relationship with them over a long period of time. This is why so many service users and carers value the care and support work role.

What do care and support workers do?

There used to be a clear distinction between the role of 'care workers' and the role of 'support workers'. Care workers traditionally carried out personal care tasks, such as helping people wash, eat and go to the toilet; support workers helped with practical tasks like budgeting, shopping and developing social networks. But these boundaries are now much more blurred.

In many services, staff who help with personal care tasks are now expected to take on 'support-like' activities, such as promoting people's independence and helping them link into other services. New work roles are being introduced that encompass care and support activities, plus many others besides. Personal assistants, for example, are employed directly by service users (or by a broker acting on their behalf) to provide whatever help the person wants and needs, not to perform a specific role.

For example:

Jemma works in a residential care home for people with a learning disability which has recently been bought by a private company called *Growing Places*. She used to help people with their personal care, occasionally organising social activities, but now spends two days a week at a conservation project with residents from six *Growing Places* services. She works alongside service users and other volunteers from the local community, clearing litter and planting trees. Her role is to support the people using the project to learn new skills and make friends.

Not what you do, but how

With all these changes in the role, it's simpler to look not at *what* care and support workers do but at *how* they do it. This is known as the 'approach' that workers or services take. It's about the particular way we work with service users.

Ways of working in health and social care are constantly changing in response to evidence about what works best and shifting expectations in society. For example, the main priority for services used to be protecting people and keeping them safe; but this contributed to people becoming institutionalised and losing the ability to do things for themselves. Today, the priority is to support people to make their own decisions and maintain their independence.

An important feature of current approaches is the extent to which a worker builds on people's abilities and strengths and what they can do, rather than focusing on their disabilities and problems and what they can't do. We use the terms 'strengths approach' and 'problem approach' for these contrasting attitudes and different ways of working.

PROBLEM APPROACH

1. People have problems that need to be diagnosed and solved by an expert.

2. Our role is to reduce, eliminate or manage the person's problems and get them back to as 'normal' a life as possible.

STRENGTHS APPROACH

1. The individual is the expert in relation to their own situation and needs.

2. Our role is to help people identify what they want to achieve and support them in putting this into action.

These two approaches form the two ends of a continuum. Most services will probably be placed somewhere in the middle but should be moving in the 'strengths' direction.

Focusing on problems		Building on strengths

There are other differences of approach within services such as being staff focused or service user focused.

For example:

In the old asylums, patients were sometimes locked out of the wards so they couldn't go back to bed and sleep during the day. This was to ensure that they slept throughout the night and didn't disturb the night staff.

This no longer happens in hospitals or residential services but staff can still slip into doing things that help them, not the service users. For example, staff may spend a lot of time in the staff office, rather than in the communal areas with service users. They may say they have an 'open door' policy but service users may feel they are 'disturbing' the workers or 'being a nuisance' if they come to the office and ask for help.

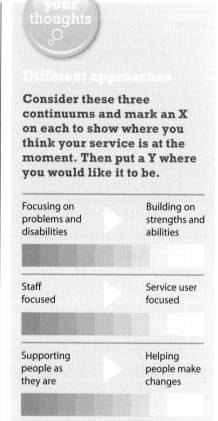

your thoughts

Different approaches

Consider these three continuums and mark an X on each to show where you think your service is at the moment. Then put a Y where you would like it to be.

Focusing on problems and disabilities		Building on strengths and abilities

Staff focused		Service user focused

Supporting people as they are		Helping people make changes

Our thoughts about this are on page 33.

How do you spend your time?

Even when we are clear about our role and how we should approach it, there may be other demands which take us away from what is important. We need to regularly review what we are doing so that we can manage our time more effectively.

Look at your job description and any other relevant documents about your role and list the three main tasks you should be doing.

1.

2.

3.

Using the table on the right, record what you actually did in a typical day or shift. Each box represents 30 minutes of your time, and there are 15 boxes for a 7.5 hour shift.

*Use the key below to describe what you **mostly** did in each 30-minute slot:*

A = Direct contact with service users

B = Activity on behalf of a service user: phone call, filling in forms etc

C = Practical task: tidying up, preparing equipment etc

D = Paperwork or record keeping

E = Meetings

F = Training activity

G = Dealing with visitors

H = Other *(describe this in the space below)*

Time chart

Time	Activity code

When you have completed your time chart look at the results and list the three activities which you spent the most time on.

Time spent (hours)	Activity code
1.	
2.	
3.	

Demands on your time

Compare how you actually spent your time with what you should have been doing. Are they the same? How are they different?

Write your thoughts here.

If your two lists are different, think about why and note the possible reasons for this here.

Our thoughts about why there may be a difference between what we should be doing and what we actually do are on page 33.

What does it mean to be good at your job?

You may feel there are so many demands in care and support work that it's really difficult to be an effective worker – to make any real difference. But if you can get to grips with the three key challenges of frontline practice you will certainly be developing in your role.

These are to:

● provide the kind of service we'd be happy to use ourselves
● work *with* service users rather than do things to or for them
● actively manage our boundaries.

The following sections will explain each of these in more detail.

Summary

The care and support worker role is an essential part of health and social care services.

To be effective in our role we need to consider how we do things, not just what we do.

The key challenges in care and support work are to provide a service we'd be happy to use ourselves; to work with service users rather than doing things to or for them and to actively manage our boundaries.

Section 2

Services we'd be happy to use

Key points

A test of a good quality service is whether we would recommend it to our friends or family, or be willing to use it ourselves.

We tend to like services that deliver *what* we want, in the *way* we want.

How we work is shaped by our values; our values influence everything we say and do.

13

'I used to dread visiting my father-in-law in the care home. He had a small, gloomy room with just enough space for a single bed and wardrobe. The floor was covered in vinyl, since he was incontinent, and an electronic air freshener squirted every half an hour. Sometimes he would be in the lounge, asleep in his chair. I'd sit next to him until he woke up, but it was so hot I often drifted off myself. The staff sometimes trundled past the door with a trolley of linen, but mostly I was just left with all the sleeping residents. From time to time one woman woke up and called for help and if nobody came she would start swearing at us. One day she threw a plastic cup of water at me.'

Would you recommend the service you work in?

The quality of health and social care services is measured by a range of different standards, including the length of waiting lists, how much the service costs and, in the case of residential care homes, for example, how clean they are. But a simple way of judging quality is to ask staff whether they would want to use the service they work in themselves.

The answer to this question will tell us a lot about the hidden factors that affect the quality of a service, which aren't easily identified in a 'tick-box' approach to measuring quality. This includes how people using services are treated. Most of us don't just want the right services to be there for us; we want to be treated in the right way.

For example:

Irene is on a weight loss programme organised through her local medical centre; she is being weighed by a nurse. The nurse says, 'You haven't lost much, have you?' Irene feels belittled and angry as she has been trying hard to exercise and eat healthily and has lost two pounds. She is also annoyed that the nurse, who is very overweight herself, speaks to her as though she's a naughty child.

If the nurse had congratulated Irene for what she had achieved, instead of focusing on what she'd failed to do, this would have encouraged her. But now Irene feels like giving up.

14

Values underpin everything we do

How we behave towards people is influenced by our values. Values are our beliefs about what is important in life, such as being kind to people or helping friends in trouble.

We need to understand the values that apply in health and social care because they guide how we behave and influence the decisions we make in our work. They also guide us when we have to make difficult choices or deal with dilemmas.

For example:

A new support worker, David, is gently explaining to a service user that lunch is ready next door and that he can help him get there. The man has dementia and doesn't understand what David is saying. David sits down next to him and tries again. Another support worker, Jackie, hurries past with a service user on each arm and calls out from across the room, 'Just take him, he'll go.' David is in a dilemma. If he does what Jackie says, he will be reinforcing bad practice by putting the convenience of staff first, but his colleagues will like him. If he ignores Jackie, he will be putting the service user first but risks annoying colleagues and making himself unpopular.

A tree of values

The values that govern health and social care work come from many different sources, including laws, policies and regulations. Because they have different roots, they are often called different things, which can be confusing for workers who are trying to put them into practice. For example, participation, empowerment and inclusion are all used in health and social care services to mean much the same thing: enabling service users to take responsibility for, and make decisions about, their own lives.

There are some core values that underpin all work with service users, whatever their age, mental and physical health, learning abilities or health and care needs.

We can think of these values as a tree. The tree trunk represents the core values from which other values emerge, like branches. At the end of the branches are all the things we do in our work that put the values into action *(see figure 1 on page 16)*.

These values shouldn't be seen in isolation. They are part of a whole approach and should all work together. For example, you can't achieve real social inclusion without also promoting equality and rights. This is why we have used the analogy of the tree. A tree with a sturdy and healthy trunk will grow well and develop healthy branches and leaves. If you get the core values right, the branches and leaves should follow.

These are some typical values:

- I believe in respecting people by being on time, therefore I try to be punctual for my appointments.
- I believe that service users should be able to talk to me about their worries, therefore I always make time to ask each person how they are.

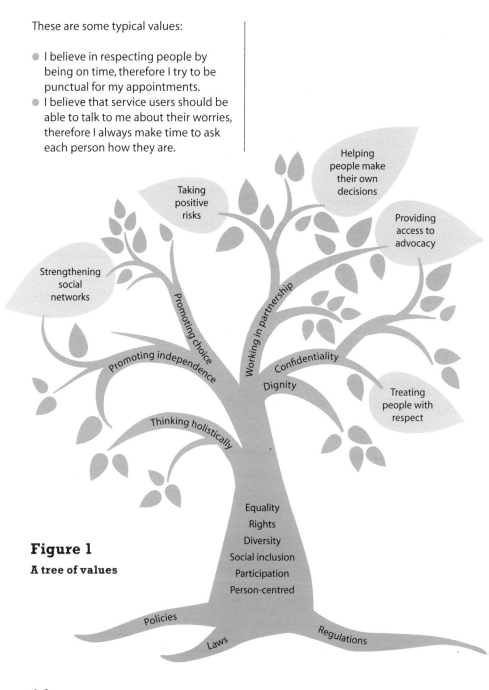

Figure 1

A tree of values

Helping people make their own decisions

Taking positive risks

Providing access to advocacy

Strengthening social networks

Promoting choice

Working in partnership

Promoting independence

Confidentiality

Dignity

Treating people with respect

Thinking holistically

Equality
Rights
Diversity
Social inclusion
Participation
Person-centred

Policies

Laws

Regulations

16

What are the three most important values for you in your work?

Fill in the blanks here:

I believe

therefore I

I believe

therefore I

I believe

therefore I

Now think about your employer or the organisation where you work. What do you think are their three most important values?

They believe

therefore they

They believe

therefore they

They believe

therefore they

What barriers prevent you from putting your values into practice?

Make a note of them here.

How does this list compare with your own list of values? Are they the same or different? How does this affect how you feel about your work?

Write your thoughts here.

Our thoughts about this are on page 33.

Problems in applying values

From time to time we see shocking media headlines about older people starving in hospitals or abuse of people in care homes. These are at the extreme end of poor practice, but many other services achieve only minimal standards of care and dignity and fail to go much beyond this. This may be because:

- workers know about the values in theory but don't know how to put them into practice
- there is a mismatch between workers' values and the values of their employer/organisation
- workers don't feel valued by managers and therefore find it hard to be positive about their work.

17

Coping strategies

Working in a poor quality service can leave us frustrated, resentful or even burnt out. Sometimes the way we cope with this can make the situation worse. For example, if we believe that our managers prioritise saving money over providing person-centred care, we may decide to do the absolute minimum required of us. As a result, our work may become less varied and interesting, and the service deteriorates further.

For example:

Megan works in a hospital ward that has just been subject to a round of cost-savings. The healthcare assistants have been told that they must run all the activity sessions because the occupational therapist (OT) post has been cut. Megan enjoyed working alongside the OT and used to bring in items from home to use in the reminiscence sessions. Now she feels angry and exploited and is refusing to do anything that is not in her job description.

Trying to improve a service requires a whole chain of people to behave differently and it may take a long time. In the meantime, we will need coping strategies to help us stay positive. As figure 2 illustrates, the first step is recognising how the situation is affecting us. Then we can devise a strategy that may have more positive outcomes for us and for service users.

The things we can control

In many work roles we may not have a choice about what we do – the particular tasks or activities that we have to carry out. But we usually have small choices about how we do things – whether we approach tasks in a more or less enabling way, for example. The choice may be small but, as we know from promoting health and well-being, it is the small things that make a difference to people's daily lives. We might not be able to improve the whole service, but we still have a responsibility to do the best we can, in ways that will make a difference to service users.

For example:

Maria has 30 minutes each morning to help Mr Stanley get out of bed, get washed and dressed. Because of the pressure of time, Maria usually grabs whatever clothes are at the top of the pile and helps him into them, whatever the weather or his plans for the day.

Melody has 30 minutes each morning to help Mr Stiles get out of bed, get washed and dressed. Because of the pressure of time, Melody has arranged with Mr Stiles that he will decide what he will wear each day, before she arrives. Melody quickly selects the clothes he's chosen from the pile, and helps him into them.

18

Figure 2
Coping strategies

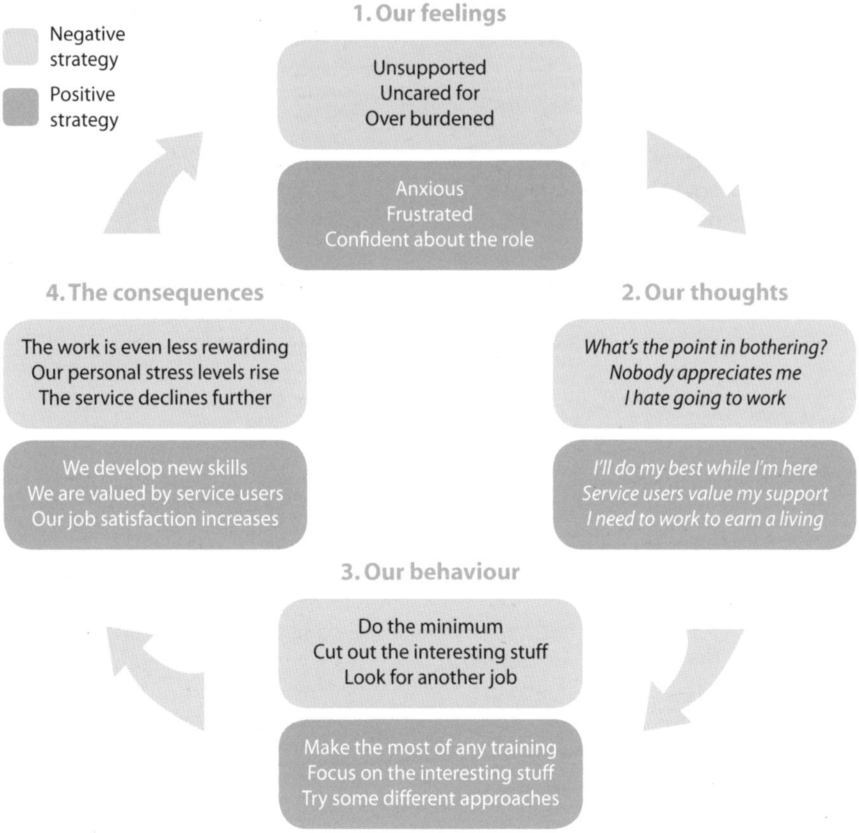

Legend:
- Negative strategy
- Positive strategy

1. Our feelings
Unsupported
Uncared for
Over burdened

Anxious
Frustrated
Confident about the role

4. The consequences
The work is even less rewarding
Our personal stress levels rise
The service declines further

We develop new skills
We are valued by service users
Our job satisfaction increases

2. Our thoughts
What's the point in bothering?
Nobody appreciates me
I hate going to work

I'll do my best while I'm here
Service users value my support
I need to work to earn a living

3. Our behaviour
Do the minimum
Cut out the interesting stuff
Look for another job

Make the most of any training
Focus on the interesting stuff
Try some different approaches

Summary

Even if we are working in a service we wouldn't want to use ourselves there are small things we can do to make things better for service users.

It can make a big difference to someone if even just one person is kind to them.

It is through our actions and behaviour that we demonstrate our true values.

19

Working with, not doing to

Key points

Working *with* people means helping them to help themselves as much as possible.

We can do this by working in partnership with them and looking for opportunities to promote choice and independence.

Small steps help people take more control over their lives and move towards bigger changes.

What does it feel like to be: **referred**; **assessed**; **reviewed**; **diagnosed**; **treated** and **discharged**?

This is some people's experience of using certain kinds of services. They feel processed, like parcels, with no control over what is happening to them. Everything is done to them as they pass through a system.

Working in partnership

Working in partnership with service users is the opposite of treating people like parcels being processed through a system. It is central to the strengths approach we described in Section 1, and one of the core health and social care values we considered in Section 2. It may not be the term that you would use because different types of services have their own language. For example, in learning disabilities services, working in partnership may be described as 'promoting independence and choice'; in mental health services it is sometimes described as 'empowerment' or 'self-management'.

In essence, working in partnership requires care and support workers to concentrate less on 'getting things done' for people, and more on 'helping people to help themselves'.

What gets in the way of partnerships?

There are many situations where people want more control over their lives and, if we want to, it is easy for workers to promote choice and independence.

There are other situations where it is more difficult because:

- it is not the usual way of doing things in the culture of that service
- workers are used to getting on and doing things for people
- service users are used to having things done for them.

For example:

Mrs Graham's home carers carry out light cleaning and laundry work and prepare her main evening meal. Mrs Graham often complains that she feels cold and a new carer, Sophia, suggests she helps with the dusting, as this would warm her up and keep her active. Mrs Graham is most put out. She says that the carers are paid to do the cleaning and Sophia should just get on with her job. Sophia knows it's easier just to do it herself so she doesn't bother mentioning it again.

21

Relationships are essential to care and support work; working in partnership with service users is about aiming, as far as possible, for a balanced and equal relationship. In the previous example, Sophia was saying, 'Let's do this *together*' but Mrs Graham regards herself as an employer who tells her staff what to do. They have different expectations of Sophia's role.

Roles in relationships

Workers have *formal* roles (for example, 'health care assistant') and *informal* roles at work (for example, 'the person in the team who always organises the social events'). Sometimes we are given an informal role which we may not always like; or we may choose to take up a particular role because it suits us. In teams, for example, you occasionally find someone who tries to 'mother' everybody and fusses about their welfare. That person may like the role because it is familiar to them and makes them feel useful.

However, too much 'mothering' of service users can become a problem. This is because, when one person acts out a particular role, the other person in the relationship is drawn into acting another role to fit with it. In the case of the 'mother', the other role is that of 'child'. Some children may rebel against being mothered and feel angry and frustrated; others may like it so much that they become even more needy. But neither of these role relationships is an equal partnership between adults.

your
thoughts

Roles we take on

Have you ever found yourself doing any of the following?
Tick all that you've tried.

☐ Trying to get someone motivated by being extra enthusiastic and energetic.

☐ Doing more for one person than you would normally do for others because you feel sorry for them.

☐ Trying to persuade a service user to do something by telling them it will be good for them: *You'll enjoy it when you get there.'*

Our thoughts about these approaches are on page 33.

Getting the right balance

True partnerships are about two people of equal status acting together to achieve a common goal. In care and support work, there is nearly always a power imbalance in the relationship between the worker and service user. For instance, we know more personal information about the service user than they know about us. The solution isn't for us to talk about our own lives the whole time. Instead, we can maintain a balance by respecting their right to exercise power in the relationship. If we don't, we may provoke an unhealthy power struggle where the service user tries to 'fight back' and get some control of a situation. This can manifest in behaviour we find challenging and service users may be labelled as 'difficult' or 'unmotivated'.

Promoting independence

Working in partnership is about trying different approaches to help people gradually take more control over aspects of their lives, as far as they are able or want. People may be more willing to take control over things that are important to them.

For example:

Mrs Graham's home carer, Sophia, has suggested that Mrs Graham helps out with some light dusting. Mrs Graham is most put out, saying that cleaning is the carers' job. Sophia explains that her role is to help Mrs Graham maintain her independence. She asks Mrs Graham what she enjoys doing and what she would like to do more of. Mrs Graham says she used to like making cakes but isn't sure she can manage it now. Sophia suggests that Mrs Graham bakes something next time Sophia comes in, so that she can help with the things Mrs Graham can't manage.

When service users resist doing more for themselves

If a person doesn't want to do something for themselves, it is their choice. But we need to be sure that we have done our best to help them, over a reasonable length of time. When someone continues to do something, or not do something, that is dangerous for their health and well-being, we have to keep trying to show them that there are other, safer ways of dealing with that particular situation. We are bound to do this by our duty of care.

Sometimes service users are called 'lazy' or 'unmotivated' because they resist doing more for themselves. It's important to avoid using labels and to try to find out what else may be going on. There are usually other factors at play. For example, the person may:

- have no confidence in their own ability
- have different expectations or standards so they don't think there is an issue or problem
- see no point in changing because they don't think their life is going to get any better.

If we understand these hidden factors we can adapt our approach to that person. However, when we are helping people to do more for themselves, there are some approaches that are worth trying and some we should try to avoid.

23

Approaches to try

- Ask what goals the person would like to achieve:
  'What would you like to be able to do more of?'
  'What's important to you?'

- Respect their goals even if you don't agree with them or think they are unrealistic:
  'I can see that's important to you.'
  'That's a good goal to have. We need to find a way of working towards it.'

- If they seem to be in two minds about a change, acknowledge it:
  'You seem to have mixed feelings about this.'

- Go for small and manageable steps with low pressure:
  'Let's just walk down to the garden gate and back and see how it goes.'
  'Let's try this today. If it doesn't work out we'll try something different tomorrow.'

- Give positive feedback when something is achieved, however small:
  'That was hard work for both of us but I think we did really well.'
  'Well done. You managed that by yourself.'

Approaches to avoid

- Avoid telling the person what you think is best for them as this tends to make people want to do the opposite:
  'If I were you I would...'
  'You should...'

- Avoid conveying the message that they are to blame or a failure, as they may already have little self-confidence:
  'How can you live like this?'
  'Look at the state of it!'

- Avoid trying to persuade them by telling them why something will be good for them:
  'You'll feel better if you take more exercise.'
  'You'll enjoy meeting new people.'

- Avoid speaking from the service's point of view:
  'We want you to be more independent.'
  'We want you to feel empowered.'

- Avoid trying to impose goals or change their goals because you don't agree with them:
  'It would be better if...'
  'I don't think that's realistic.'

Summary

Care and support work is about helping people achieve their own goals and aspirations.

Your role is to help people make their own decisions even if you don't agree with them.

Small steps are important and necessary in the journey towards independence.

Managing our boundaries

Key points

Managing our work boundaries means not stepping over the line between acceptable and unacceptable behaviour at work.

If we step outside our work boundaries we may cause considerable distress to service users.

If we step outside our work boundaries we may put ourselves or the service user at risk of harm and may face disciplinary action.

'I was 21 when I started working in mental health and I really had no idea what I was doing. The rest of the team were about the same age and we used to have a lot of fun at work and socialise together. I remember that one day a patient came up to me and started talking to me about some really embarrassing things that I'd been up to in my private life. I was really shocked. I never considered that the patients took any notice of us! No wonder he didn't see anything wrong with talking about my private life. I'd put it all on display.'

What are boundaries?

In health and social care, the term 'boundaries'refers to the dividing line between acceptable behaviour and unacceptable behaviour. Boundaries are needed to:

● protect workers
● protect service users, and
● help everyone feel safe.

If you have ever been in a situation where someone crosses your boundaries you will know how confusing and unsettling it can be.

Relationships with service users

There are clear rules about our relationships with service users that set very clear boundaries around our behaviour. For example, it is not acceptable in any circumstances to get drunk at work or borrow money from or have sex with people using our services. If we break these rules we will be disciplined and, in some circumstances, we could face legal action.

However, there are other relationship boundaries at work that are less clear-cut because people don't always behave in predictable ways.

For example:

Sarah works in a drop-in centre. One of the regular service users, Jakko, often says she is beautiful, and this is a running joke with the other workers. Jakko arrives at the centre this morning proudly displaying a large tattoo of Sarah's name across his forearm. Other service users and workers are teasing Jakko about this but Sarah is completely freaked out and doesn't know what to do.

In the example of Jakko getting the tattoo, for instance, no organisation would have a policy or procedure to guide workers in dealing with this particular situation. So, we need to think about and actively manage our work boundaries to avoid getting into difficult situations.

How boundaries get blurred

Boundaries often become blurred when people have different expectations of each other.

For example:

Milly is a home carer for Mrs Godfrey who has just been admitted to hospital in an emergency. None of the neighbours are willing to look after Mrs Godfrey's dog and social services cannot help so Milly reluctantly takes the dog home with her. When Mrs Godfrey returns from hospital two weeks later, she makes a complaint against Milly saying that the dog hasn't been fed properly. Milly is furious as she was only trying to help, and looking after the dog was a complete nightmare.

Even if the main pressure to overstep your boundaries is coming from another person, or is due to factors beyond your control, you can still do your best to make sure you maintain your own boundaries. This will protect you and other people. One key way in which you can maintain clear

your thoughts

Think about a difficult relationship that you have had with a service user. What was tricky about this relationship? What did that person do that you found difficult to cope with?

How did this affect you?

Our thoughts about these difficult relationships are on page 34.

boundaries is by making sure you do not slip from a professional relationship into a personal one with a service user.

The difference between professional and personal relationships

Our relationships with our friends and family are private and personal. We can choose our friends and the type of relationship we have with them – how often we see them, for example, the level of intimacy we have, and what we do for them. If we get fed up with our friends we can ignore them.

27

Work relationships are different. Our job description and job role decide for us who we work with and what we do together – whether we like it or not.

PERSONAL RELATIONSHIPS

- We are accountable to each other.
- They are regulated by social norms, expectations and manners.
- They meet both people's personal needs.

PROFESSIONAL RELATIONSHIPS

- We are accountable to our manager and the organisation.
- They are regulated by policies, procedures and the law.
- Their sole focus is to promote the well-being of the service user.

The intimacy of care and support work may sometimes blur the difference between personal and professional relationships. We often do 'home-like' things with service users, sometimes in their own home. But even when we are working with people in an intimate way or with very personal issues, it is still a working relationship. No relationship with a service user is a personal one.

your thoughts

Personal v professional relationships

Which of the following are acceptable in a) a personal relationship and b) a work relationship with a service user?

Tick A or B:

A = *Acceptable in a **personal** relationship*
B = *Acceptable in a **work** relationship with a service user*

	A	B
1. Offering your own money to help someone out		
2. Talking about your own problems		
3. Selling them items from a catalogue that earns you commission		
4. Inviting them to join your on-line network as a friend		
5. Getting into bed together to watch television		
6. Giving out your personal telephone number		

Our thoughts about whether these behaviours are acceptable in a working relationship are on page 34.

28

Intimacy and touch

One way in which we can keep relationships professional is by being extra alert to issues around intimacy and how we manage personal space. Our personal space is the invisible area around our body that determines how close another person can get without making us feel uncomfortable. The size of our personal space depends on lots of factors, including our culture and gender, and it changes according to the situation we are in. For example, if we get into a crowded lift we accept being pressed up against strangers because we want to get to our destination as soon as possible. We know the situation won't last long and can guess that other people are feeling just as uncomfortable. But if we are in an empty lift (or a wide open space) and a stranger comes and presses up against us, we would feel extremely threatened.

Boundaries around touch

The size of our personal space also changes with our mood. If we are angry, for example, we usually want people to keep away, which means our personal space gets bigger. Some people invade someone else's personal space deliberately to intimidate them – hence the phrase, 'He was in my face'. Others have no sense of personal space at all and no idea that they might be invading ours. For example, sexual abuse during childhood sometimes leads adults to be very confused about boundaries and personal space.

This complexity of personal space is why touch is so tricky. Touch can make people feel angry, threatened, sexually aroused, or comforted. What we intend may not be how a person experiences our touch. Therefore it is generally best not to touch service users unless it is necessary to help with a personal care task. Personal care is a bit like the lift scenario: although it can be embarrassing and stressful, both parties know that it has a specific purpose and will end. There are some other situations where it may be appropriate to touch – such as holding a hand to reassure or comfort someone – but we can never make assumptions that it will be experienced positively.

Strategies to help us manage our boundaries

The quote at the beginning of this section was from a worker who said that she didn't understand much about her role when she started her first job. Nobody explained to her about boundaries and this was partly because her colleagues were also unaware of their importance. There are three strategies we can use to help us take an active approach to keeping boundaries in place:

- Having a 'work face'.
- Being assertive.
- Taking time to reflect on relationships.

'Home face'/'work face'

One way to manage the difference between our personal self and our work self is to have a work persona – to conceal the 'real us' when we're at work.

29

The person we are at work will not be the same as the person we are with friends and family. That person will dress and behave differently.

We need to go through a process between home and work where we put on our work face and take it off again when we leave. In fact, many workers do this without being aware of it; for example by having a shower and literally 'washing off' work when they get home.

One very clear way in which services mark the difference between the personal and professional is by expecting staff to wear a uniform. This has pros and cons.

For example it may:

- help service users feel confident about the professionalism of the staff
- help staff put on their work face as they get ready for work.

But it may also:

- be seen as institutional and create a barrier between staff and service users
- stop staff being seen as individuals – the opposite to what we want to achieve in person-centred care.

The disadvantages have led many services to abandon uniforms but this can create some tricky boundary issues about what clothes are appropriate for work.

your thoughts

Boundaries around clothing

Micky works in a hostel for homeless men who are recovering from alcohol-related problems. During a hot summer, Micky comes to work wearing a vest top and very brief shorts. The service manager tells him this is inappropriate clothing but is unable to explain why.

Micky points out that all the staff are wearing informal clothes, including shorts, and that what he wears is part of his identity.

Why could Micky's clothes be seen as inappropriate?

What kind of problems could be caused by Micky wearing these clothes?

Our thoughts about clothing are on page 34.

Assertiveness skills

There are some situations where we need to assert a boundary very clearly by saying 'No'. This includes saying no when:

- we are asked to do something beyond the limits of our role
- someone is treating us badly or abusing us
- we feel unsafe.

Many of us find it hard to say no and have developed ways of getting round it; for example, by avoiding certain people, going off sick from work, or making promises that we do not intend to keep.

Assertiveness is about communicating our needs, wants and feelings while respecting other people's right to do the same. Learning how to be more assertive doesn't guarantee that you will get what you want, but it will help you make your boundaries clear. When we are clear about our boundaries people are less likely to constantly test them.

Reflecting on relationships

It is hard to be objective about any kind of relationship so we usually need help from other people to reflect on our relationships at work. We can get this through supervision, but if you don't have this type of support, here are three other ways of making space for reflection about work relationships:

- Have a short offloading time at the end of meetings, such as handovers, where anyone can talk about what's on their mind.
- Keep a notebook to write down your thoughts and feelings and what you notice about relationships with people.
- On the way home from work, think about one thing that went well that day and one thing that didn't go well and how you could do things differently next time.

One of the benefits of making time for reflection is that you are less likely to carry negative feelings home with you – another part of the process of taking off your work face.

Note: *The subject of assertiveness is too big to address fully here but there is more information in the Resources section on the Realife Learning website at:* **www.realifelearning.co.uk**

Summary

Working relationships and personal relationships are very different and should be kept separate.

Developing a 'work face' is a useful strategy for maintaining healthy work boundaries while still behaving like a real person with service users

Relationships can be complex and confusing so we need to make time to think about boundaries and develop our assertiveness skills.

31

In this section we set out **our** ideas about the 'your thoughts' exercises featured throughout this booklet and tell you how you can access other resources to help you carry on improving in your role as a frontline worker.

These are our ideas in response to the 'your thoughts' exercises:

(page 08)
Promoting well-being

Promoting well-being means finding out what is important to each person we're working with, building on their strengths, abilities and interests and helping them do the things they are good at, or that they enjoy. The emphasis is on simple activities so, in practice, this may mean helping someone to prepare a favourite meal, listen to some music or contact a friend.

(page 10)
Different approaches

The trend in health and social care is towards ensuring people have more choice and control – the strengths approach. Where you locate your service on the continuum will depend on how quickly it has adapted to this trend.

(page 12)
Demands on your time

There are different reasons why there can be a mismatch between what we do and what we're supposed to be doing. For example:

- Work roles and job descriptions may change, but workers often carry on doing the same things.
- Constant interruptions can prevent workers getting on with their work unless there are strategies in place to deal with this.

(page 17)
Conflicting values

If there is a mismatch in values we may find ourselves getting into trouble at work or feeling very stressed. We may also resort to coping strategies that have a negative impact on service users and lead to an inconsistent service. For example:

- Pretending to go along with what we are told, but doing what we were going to do anyway.
- Distancing ourselves from the work and doing the minimum required.

(page 22)
Roles we take on

Trying to get someone motivated by being extra enthusiastic and energetic.
This cheerleader role may work in the short term but you'll end up exhausted and will probably irritate the other person.

Doing more for someone than you would normally do for others because you feel sorry for them.
This is a bit like a 'mothering' role and runs the risk of making people more dependent or resentful.

Trying to persuade a service user to do something by telling them that it will be good for them: 'You'll enjoy it when you get there.'
This 'look on the bright side' approach is unlikely to be effective because it is your view, not theirs. The person needs to identify the benefits of something for themselves, and your role is to help them do that.

33

(page 27)
Difficult relationships

Many difficult relationships involve problems with setting boundaries. For example:

● Finding it hard to say 'no' to someone.
● Stopping behaviour that we experience as abusive.
● Responding to someone who is very needy.

Helping people learn about boundaries may be an explicit part of our job role; or we may feel that boundary problems get in the way of our 'real work'. Either way it is part and parcel of care and support work with people.

(page 28)
Personal v professional relationships

None of these actions are acceptable in a working relationship with service users. They all cross the boundaries of a professional relationship.

(page 30)
Boundaries around clothing

We all have different views about what 'suitable clothing' looks like, depending on our personal taste, age and sexual orientation, for example. So it's not surprising that Micky's manager –who wears chino trousers and a buttoned-up shirt to work– finds it difficult to explain his view.

Wearing revealing clothes at work can cross a boundary by sending out unintended sexual invitations such as 'Look at my body' or 'Come and get me'.

Other resources

We hope you have found this booklet useful. If you would like more practice in the skills needed to develop in your professional role, we have produced other resources that may help you. These are:

● Managing difficult boundaries
● Practising assertion skills

There are two ways that you can link to these resources:

Our website
Go to our website at **www.realifelearning.co.uk** and click on the Resources section.

QR code
Scan the QR code with your smartphone to go to our website and click on the Resources section.

QR codes are two-dimensional barcodes that contain hidden information like text or web addresses. To use QR codes you will need a QR reader which you can download free from many app providers.

frontline practice series

Discover more booklets in this series which will help you develop your knowledge and skills in other real life situations at:
www.realifelearning.co.uk

34